Short ^ish Walks
near Taunton

Robert Hesketh

Bossiney Books

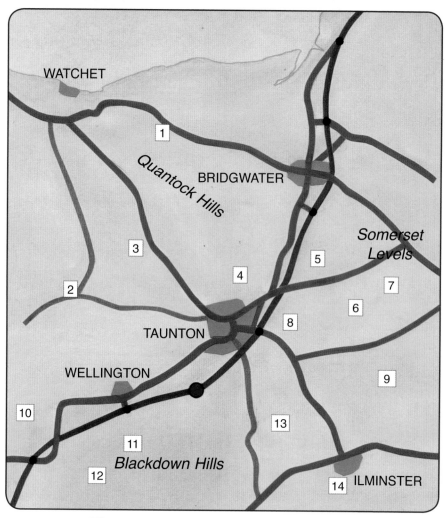

The approximate locations of the walks in this book

First published 2015 by
Bossiney Books Ltd, 33 Queens Drive, Ilkley, LS29 9QW
www.bossineybooks.com

© 2015 Robert Hesketh All rights reserved
ISBN 978-1-906474-49-2

Acknowledgements
The maps are by Graham Hallowell. The boots on the front cover were kindly
supplied by The Brasher Boot Company. All photographs are by the author.

Printed in Great Britain by Latimer Trend & Company Ltd, Plymouth

2

Introduction

The routes in this book have been chosen to help you explore the beautiful and varied countryside around Taunton, embracing the Quantocks, the Blackdown Hills and the Levels as well as the Vale of Taunton. All are within 20 km/13 miles of the town, and several are on regular bus routes. Lengths vary from 5 km/3 miles up to 9.6 km/6 miles, so the time needed to complete them will vary. Some are level, others are a bit more challenging, but why hurry? There are many wonderful viewpoints and places of interest to linger over on the way and every walk has its individual character.

Footwear and clothing

Walking is a pleasure throughout the seasons so long as you're prepared. There will be some mud at most times of the year and perhaps a lot of mud and puddles in winter and after rain, especially on the Levels and riverbank walks. Walking boots are ideal, but sandals inadequate, whilst Wellingtons don't breathe or provide ankle support.

It's sensible to take extra layers of clothing as well as a waterproof for our changeable climate. On some paths there may be gorse or nettles, so it's wise to carry a walking stick. Equally, trousers are preferable to shorts, especially as they provide some protection against ticks which may carry Lyme disease. If a tick does attach itself to you, remove it promptly and carefully with tweezers.

Extras

Drinking water is a must – you will soon need it and dehydration causes tiredness. Take a mobile phone if you have one. The sketch maps in this book are just that – sketches. You may want to carry an OS Explorer map (numbers 140 and 128 cover the territory) for extra information.

The countryside

Walking is safe and healthy exercise, but please watch out for uneven and waterlogged ground. Despite many pressures on their livelihoods, farmers are still trying to make a living from the land you will pass through. Please respect their crops. Stay on the paths, leave gates closed or open as you find them, and keep dogs under control, especially during the lambing and bird nesting season and in nature reserves.

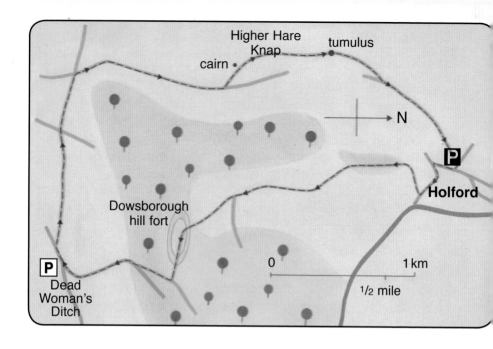

Higher Hare Knap

tumulus

cairn

N

P

Holford

Dowsborough hill fort

P

Dead Woman's Ditch

0   1 km

¹/2 mile

Walk 1 Holford, Dowsborough and Hare Knap

Distance: 7.8 km/4³/4 miles   Map 140
Character: This exploration of Quantock's eastern flank gives fine
views over the Bristol Channel and Bridgwater Bay. It includes an Iron
Age hill fort and follows a section of the Herepath, one of King Alfred's
military roads. There is one long but steady ascent and descent.

Quantock is criss-crossed with unofficial paths and animal tracks, so
careful attention to the directions and map are needed.

Turn right out of Holford's Bowling Green car park, facing towards the village. Turn right only 100 m ahead and then turn left after another 80 m at the Triangle. Follow the lane up and over the brow of the hill to a waymark inscribed QUANTOCK RIDGEWAY.

Turn right and follow the bridleway uphill through a gate. When the path divides, keep left and continue past a cairn on your right and thence uphill. Keep ahead at a path junction and continue uphill on the public bridleway to the rampart of Dowsborough hill fort.

Turn left and follow the path with the rampart on your left. Before invasive trees grew here, the 340 m elevation gave defenders extensive views and ample warning of any visitors, friendly or otherwise. The rampart encloses a substantial 2.7 ha (6¹/2 acres) and would, with its

4

complementary ditch, have been considerably higher when first built, before erosion by more than 2000 years of rain and wind.

Leave the rampart and continue to a cross track. Turn right and follow the track down to a lane, ignoring side turnings. Turn right up the lane, part of the Herepath or Anglo-Saxon military road which ran from Cannington over Quantock and on across the Brendons and Exmoor. (See page 28 for another herepath.) Follow it as it curves right and continue to the signpost marked DEAD WOMAN'S DITCH – the ditch possibly being an outer defence for the hill fort.

Bear right (CROWCOMBE) then right onto a signed bridleway 80 m ahead. Follow the bridleway for 800 m to a cross track. Continue for another 400 m along the broad ridge track.

Turn right along a clear track heading north towards the brow of a hill. When the track divides, turn left to the cairn on Higher Hare Knap – a fine viewpoint.

Head north and downhill on a broad grassy path and then up the low rise ahead, which is crowned with a ruined tumulus (prehistoric burial mound).

Follow the track downhill. Merge with another track and continue downhill through a gate. The path divides only 20 m ahead. Keep left. Continue downhill past a cottage and ahead as signed to the car park.

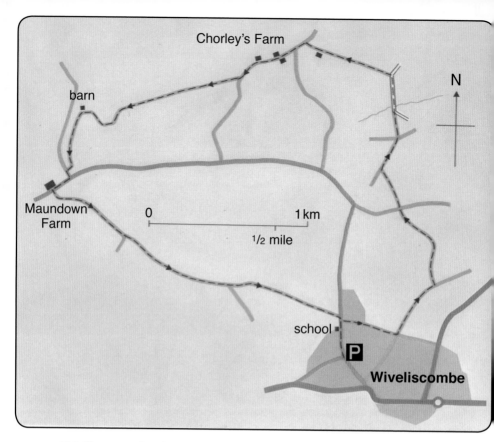

Walk 2 Wiveliscombe

Distance: 7.4 km (4³/4 miles) Map 128
Character: A scenic walk in the Brendon Hills from Wiveliscombe, with its pleasing medley of mainly Georgian and Victorian buildings. There are several slopes, but none long or arduous. Parts muddy after rain.

Turn right out of the signed car park in North Street. Follow the road past the school. Turn right, NORTHGATE. Turn left into PUBLIC FOOTPATH between a house and a wall just 20 m before reaching a junction.

Follow the enclosed path to a stile. Here, the footpath divides. Keep left. Cross a second stile and a field to a third stile and continue ahead with the hedge on your left over two more stiles. Continue along the enclosed path to a lane.

Cross and continue ahead (PUBLIC FOOTPATH) past a barn on the right. Continue with the hedge on your left. The path bends right.

6

Go through a gate and follow the lane to a junction. Cross a stile and follow the PUBLIC FOOTPATH downhill to a bridge. Follow the track uphill for 250 m.

Turn left up steps and immediately right over a stile, PUBLIC FOOTPATH. Now facing west, cross the field ahead to a gate. Continue across the next field and over a stile. Continue past a house to a lane.

Turn left, then after 30 m go straight ahead when the road turns left. Continue past Chorley's Farmhouse. Turn right over a stile and cross the large field ahead to another stile. Cross a small field to a gate. Continue along a short enclosed path. Turn right and follow the right field edge to a barn.

Follow the right field edge to a stile. Leave by a gate at the end of the next field. Turn left onto the lane and almost immediately right and uphill.

Turn left opposite Maundown Farm. Follow the lane uphill to a junction. Fork left, PUBLIC BRIDLEWAY.

When the path divides, keep left, PUBLIC BRIDLEWAY. Continue downhill, enjoying views over Wiveliscombe. Reaching North Street, turn right and walk past the school to the start.

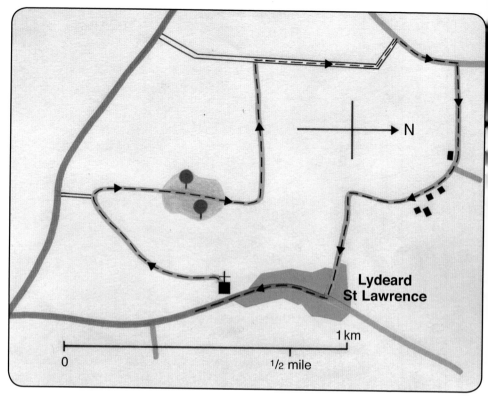

Walk 3   Lydeard St Lawrence

Distance: 4.8 km/3 miles   Map 140
Character: This gentle walk uses footpaths and quiet lanes and offers views onto the Quantocks. It is centred on the attractive village of Lydeard St Lawrence, with its handsome red sandstone church, historic farmhouses and cottages.

Start from the roadside parking area by the church and school. Walk towards the church and turn left into the churchyard, signed as a footpath. The church has many interesting features, including a studded oak door; carved capitals; a fine screen and pulpit.

 Leave the churchyard via a kissing gate at the far side. Bear diagonally left across the field as signed to a stile. Continue in the same direction down to a steel gate and then diagonally left across the next field. Reaching the far corner, turn right and head north with the field edge on your left. Leave the field just right of the top far corner by way of a stile. Follow the woodland path ahead. Look out for deer slots in the soft earth and enjoy the bluebells in spring.

Leave the wood by a stile at the far end. Continue ahead, parallel to the stream. Turn left across the footbridge. Follow the path ahead to a stile. Turn immediately left through a gate and then immediately right over another stile. Keep the field edge on your right. Cross a stile and continue ahead, keeping a wooded field margin and then a line of trees on your right.

Cross a stile and turn right into an enclosed track. Continue on the track when it curves left. Reaching a lane, turn right.

Take the next lane right, LYDEARD ST LAWRENCE. Follow the lane as it bends sharp right by Westowe Farmhouse. Continue as the lane bends sharp left. Reaching a junction, turn right and follow the village main street to the start.

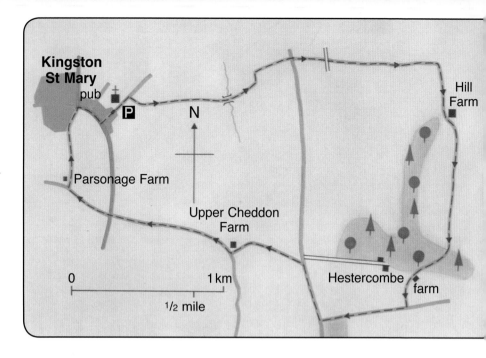

Walk 4 Kingston St Mary

Distance: 8.3 km/5¼ miles Map 140 or map 128
Character: This pleasing pastoral walk uses field paths, bridleways
and quiet lanes and offers a variety of views and scenery. Parts may
be somewhat overgrown in summer and attention to directions and
waymarks is needed, especially where the bridleway has been diverted
between Volis Cottages and Hill Farm.

Start from the car park opposite St Mary's (or park carefully on
Church Lane during church services). Turn right out of the car park.
After 40 m, turn right, PUBLIC FOOTPATH VOLIS. Cross a stile. Follow
the footpath through a wood.

Leave by a stile and cross the next two fields as signed. Continue
over a footbridge to the top left corner of the next field. Cross the stile
and turn left, following the left field edge to a lane.

Continue ahead, PUBLIC BRIDLEWAY. (This section had been recently
diverted at the time of writing.) Leave the first field by a metal gate.
Cross the track and continue ahead as signed to a gate at the far corner
of the field. Bear diagonally left as signed, aiming for a metal gate by
the far hedge. Follow the field edge as signed through a series of three
gates into a woodland path.

The path skirts Hill Farm to your left. Continue through a metal gate as signed. Bear right and aim for the stile in the middle of the hedge opposite. Cross a stile and continue ahead along the right field edge into a woodland track. Turn right at a track junction. Continue past a farmhouse to a lane.

Turn right (HESTERCOMBE GARDENS) and right again at the next lane junction, HESTERCOMBE GARDENS. Reaching Park Gate, either continue 50 m ahead and divert right to visit Hestercombe Gardens, or turn left, KINGSTON ST MARY. Follow the lane past Upper Cheddon Farm to Mill Cross.

Cross the road and continue ahead FULFORD. At Parsonage Farm turn right, PUBLIC FOOTPATH VILLAGE. Continue past a house along a field edge and into an enclosed path. Turn right past the Swan Inn. Take the second turn left (CHURCH LANE) to the car park.

Hestercombe Gardens
Covering 21 ha (50 acres), Hestercombe includes Georgian and Victorian gardens, as well as gardens designed by Sir Edwin Lutyens and Gertrude Jekyll. Other attractions include a gallery, a watermill, a children's area and a café/restaurant. Open all year (except Christmas Day). 01823 413923, admission charge.

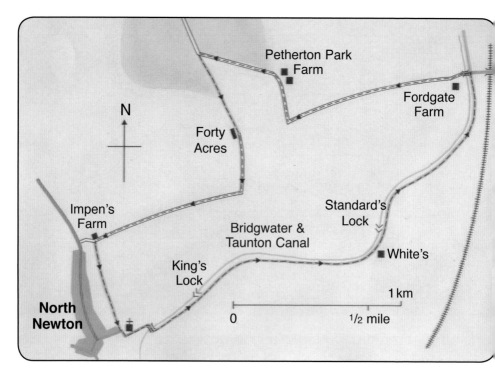

Walk 5   North Newton

Distance: 7.7 km/4³/₄ miles Map 140
Character: A level, easy walk using the towpath of the Bridgwater &
Taunton Canal, field paths, farm tracks and lanes.

Park carefully on CHURCH ROAD. Facing the church tower, follow
CHURCH ROAD as it bends right by the church and then left. Cross the
canal bridge and turn left.

Follow the canal towpath past King's Lock and Standard's Lock.
Continue to Fordgate and turn left over the bridge.

Follow the track through a metal gate to a barn. Bear right (PUBLIC
FOOTPATH) up a broad track.

At Petherton Park Farm the track bends sharp left. Continue ahead
on the track, but when it bends sharp right, turn left and follow the
field edge with the hedge and an orchard on your right, under the
power lines. At the end of the field cross the stile and continue in the
same direction past the deserted barns at Forty Acres.

Continue on the track when it bends sharp right. Turn sharp left at
Impen's Farm between stone buildings as signed. Continue along the

12

field edge with the hedge on your right and bear right towards farm buildings as signed. Follow the track to the church.

The Bridgwater & Taunton Canal
The canal was opened in 1827 and was intended to link with the Grand Western Canal (page 23), plus the rivers Exe and Parrett to make a continuous waterway between the Bristol and English Channels. Before that dream could be realised for canal barges, the railways came to Somerset and decline set in on the canal. Commercial traffic ended in 1907, but leisure use continues.

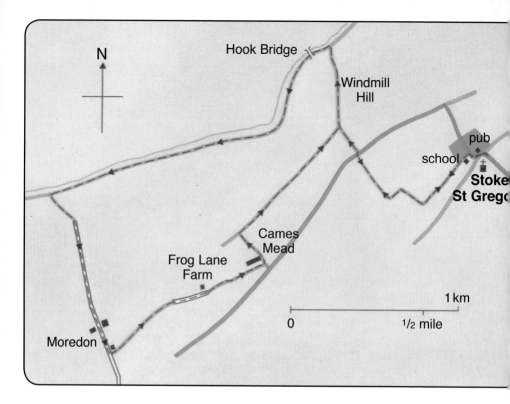

Walk 6   Stoke St Gregory and Curload

Distance: 8.5 km/5 1/4 miles   Map 128
*Character: Although mainly level, this walk offers a fine panorama
from Windmill Hill. The riverside path includes Currymoor SSSI, a
haven for wetland plants and wildfowl, including redshank, curlew,
swan, heron and mallard. This walk should be avoided after heay rain
as Currymoor can flood, especially in winter. Please check local weather
reports if in doubt.*

Park in the village square, near to the church. Facing the Royal Oak,
turn left and follow WILLEY ROAD as it bends right. Immediately past
the school turn left, PUBLIC FOOTPATH. Continue past houses and left
of allotments, then along the left edge of a field. At the field corner
turn right then left over a footbridge.

Turn right and follow the field to the corner and then left to a stile
on the right. Cross and follow the right field edge. At the end of the
field continue along the left edge of the next field to the road. Turn
right and almost immediately left, PUBLIC FOOTPATH.

Turn right at the top of the rise. Go through a metal gate and continue with the hedge on your right to Windmill Hill. A plaque explains the history of milling and various landmarks. The views stretch from the Wellington Monument, 21 km (13 miles) west to Glastonbury Tor, 20 km (13 miles) east. Follow the right field edge steeply downhill to a path junction. Turn left then right around the back of farm buildings. Cross the small field ahead.

Turn left onto the riverside track and continue on the south bank past Hook Bridge. Follow the riverbank path through Currymoor SSSI.

Stop at a metal gate signed EAST DEANE WAY. Turn sharp left and cut diagonally left across the meadow to another metal gate. Continue ahead (EAST DEANE WAY) up the low ridge ahead, past a house. Just past a brick bungalow turn left (EAST DEANE WAY) and follow the signed path. Join an enclosed track, which becomes a lane.

Turn left at CAMES MEAD. Go through the farmyard and continue along the left edge of a field as signed, joining a track to reach a metal gate. Turn right. Keep the hedge on your right to a stile. Continue ahead, following the EAST DEANE WAY signs via fields and stiles, ignoring side turnings.

Continue to the point where you earlier turned right for Windmill Hill. Turn right and retrace your steps to the start.

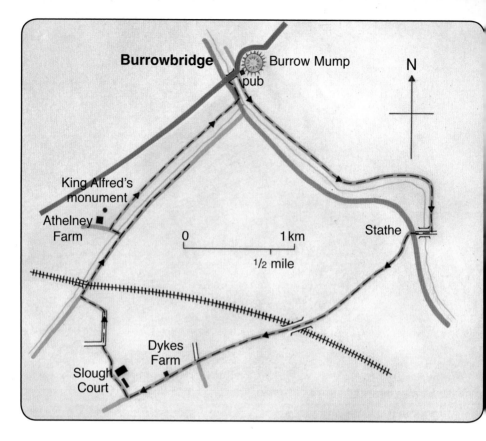

Walk 7   Stathe and Burrow Mump

Distance: 9.6 km/6 miles   Map 128 and map 140
Character: This route combines riverbank paths with quiet lanes
and field paths. Although long, it is largely level with only very mild
inclines.

Park carefully on the lane near Stathe Bridge. With your back to the
bridge follow the lane past a series of cottages and farms. Continue
over the railway bridge. At the crossroads continue ahead, past Dykes
Farm.

   Turn right, PUBLIC FOOTPATH. Walk past a barn and turn left into a
field. Follow the right field edge past Slough Court, originally a forti-
fied late medieval manor house. Cross rough ground to a stile. Turn
right and then left 100 m ahead. Follow the track down the centre of
the field. Leave by a gate. Follow the drove to a footbridge. Continue
along the left field edge to a lane.

16

Turn right over the railway. Turn left at the next junction, LYNG DURLSTON. Cross the bridge and turn right up the riverbank path.

The footpath meets the lane at Stanmoor Bridge. Cross the lane and continue ahead on the riverside path. Enjoy the view of Burrow Mump.

Cross the arched bridge. Unless you wish to visit the Mump by walking 100 m along the road and turning right up steps, turn immediately right by the King Alfred. Simply follow the delightful riverbank path back to Stathe. Cross Stathe Bridge and continue to the start.

Burrow Mump
Burrow Mump is a natural outcrop of Keuper Marl which was probably further raised artificially. Occupied during the Roman period, it has had many uses: a lookout for King Alfred's forces in 878; the site of a Norman castle; a medieval chapel and a Royalist redoubt during the Civil War. The existing ruins are mainly 18th century rebuilds.

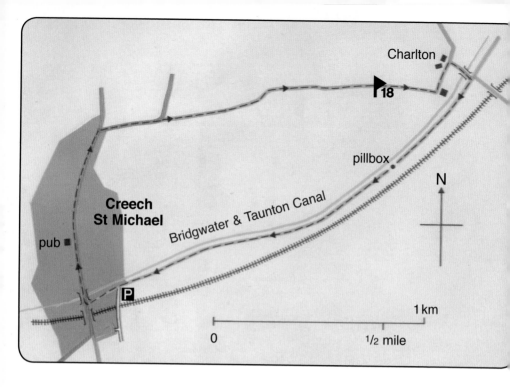

Walk 8   Creech St Michael

Distance: 5.1 km/3 1/4 miles   Map 128
Character: This easy, level walk uses footpaths lanes and tracks and
includes a pleasant section of the Bridgwater & Taunton Canal.
Start from the canal side car park, signed from Creech St Michael.

Turn left onto the canal towpath at the far end of the car park. When
you reach the road bridge, turn right. Follow the pavement past the
Bell Inn and continue to a mini roundabout.

Turn right, NORTH END. Bear right into WORTHY LANE. Ignore side
turnings and continue ahead along the gravel path and onto a grassy
track. Cross a stile. Turn left and follow the field edge, keeping the
hedge on your left. Stay with the hedge when it turns sharp right, but
leave it behind when it turns sharp left and continue straight across
the field to a stile at the far side. Cross the stile and follow the enclosed
path onto a golf course. Cross the golf course carefully as signed
(beware flying balls!) and leave it at the far end by a stile.

Follow the enclosed path to a lane. Turn right. Cross the bridge and
turn right. Simply follow the towpath back to the start.

There is much of interest on the way. Look out for the pillbox –
the canal was, like the Taunton/Chard branch railway (page 30),
part of the 'Taunton Stop Line' during the Second World War.
Look out too for the nearby converted Engine House, which
dates from 1826. The canal is a haven for many birds, including
swan, mallard, heron and moorhen. It also supports an
abundance of wildflowers such as iris and water lily, as well as
insects – dragonflies and damselflies in particular.

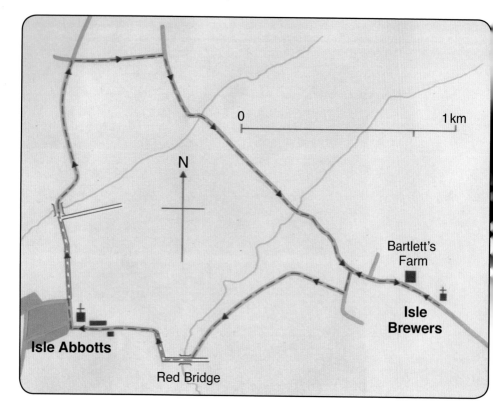

Walk 9   Isle Brewers and Isle Abbotts

Distance: 5.8 km/3³/₄ miles   Map 128
Character: This easy, level route follows field paths and quiet lanes to link two attractive villages, with their pleasing medley of limestone and Ham stone masonry, tile and thatch.

Use the roadside parking area by the post box 150 m west of Isle Brewers church. Walk west along the lane (away from the church) past Bartlett's Farm. Take the first lane left. Turn right, PUBLIC FOOTPATH. Follow it along a track and through a gate as signed. Follow the path across a field and turn left past a dewpond.

Leave the field by a stile. Do not cross the footbridge on your right. Continue straight ahead along the right field edge. Leave by a metal gate. Bear right, keeping the watercourse on your right.

Turn right over Red Bridge along a track. Follow the track right over a cattle grid. The track bends left and continues to Isle Abbotts. Divert right to visit the beautiful Ham stone church, noted for its 26 m/81 ft

20

tall tower and elegant proportions. There is much of interest inside, including the Norman font, the carved ceiling bosses and a stone coffin.

Continue up the lane. When it curves sharp left, follow the track ahead, PUBLIC FOOTPATH FIVEHEAD. Go through a metal gate and across a footbridge. Follow the right field edge. Bear diagonally left across the next field and straight on as signed.

Turn right ISLE BREWERS WESTPORT on reaching a lane. Turn right again at the next junction, ISLE BREWERS WESTPORT. Simply follow the lane back to the start.

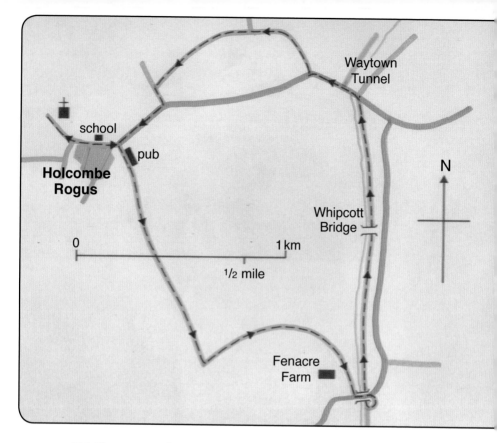

Walk 10 Holcombe Rogus

Distance: 5.8 km/3³/4 miles Map 128
Character: This gentle walk from the attractive village of Holcombe
Rogus includes a section of the 200 year old Grand Western Canal,
noted for its wild flowers and birds.

Park carefully in the main village street close to the church, which makes a delightful group with 16th century Holcombe Court and the medieval church house (now Priest's House). From the church, walk back to the main street and turn left. Follow the street past the school.

Turn right by the garage PUBLIC FOOTPATH. Walk past the Prince of Wales and follow the footpath through a farmyard. Continue along the farm track. Go through a gate and walk across the field as signed. Reaching the far edge of the field, turn left and follow the field edge with the wood on your right. Leave the field via a gate at the far end and follow the enclosed path ahead. Cross a footbridge and continue

in the same direction with the stream on your right. The stream curves right and so does the path. Continue to a lane.

Turn left over the bridge and immediately right down to the canal towpath. Turn right and follow the towpath under Fenacre Bridge. Continue under Whipcott Bridge and the former wharf and past the Waytown limekilns on the opposite bank. A plaque explains how limestone was brought from nearby quarries until the late 19th century and resulting burnt lime shipped along the canal.

Walk up the ramp at Waytown Tunnel and turn left onto the lane, HOLCOMBE ROGUS. Turn right onto a narrow lane. Continue ahead at the next junction. Turn left at the following junction and shortly afterwards right, HOLCOMBE ROGUS. Continue into the main village street past the school to the start.

Grand Western Canal

The Grand Western Canal was intended to link the English and Bristol Channels, but the arrival of the Bristol to Exeter railway in 1844 hit canal traffic hard and only the Tiverton to Lowdswells Tunnel section was cut; that beyond to Taunton being only a tub boat channel. Now used for recreation, the canal and its towpath are rich in historic interest, including bridges, milestones, wharves and limekilns.

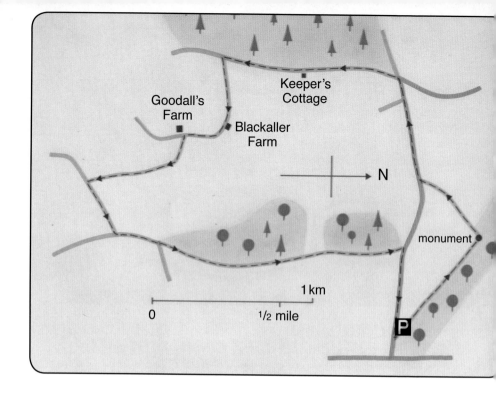

Walk 11 Wellington Monument

Distance: 7.1 km/4¹/₂ miles Map 128
Character: Using footpaths and quiet lanes, this walk explores the fields and woods around the striking 53 m (175 ft) tall Wellington Monument and offers extensive views.

Follow the broad path from the far end of the signed National Trust car park to the monument. Take the path heading south-west away from the monument. Cross a stile and continue along the field edge with beeches on your right. Leave by a stile 100 m to the left of the bottom right field corner.

Turn right onto the road. Ignore the first junction. Take the second turn on the left, CULMSTOCK. Then take the first turn left, BLACKALLER FARM. Continue past Blackaller Farm.

Just before reaching another farm, turn left and downhill, PUBLIC FOOTPATH. The path bends right by barns and continues through a gate. Cross two fields as signed, into an orchard.

Turn left up the lane by the entrance to Culmpyne Barton. Turn left

24

at the next junction and continue uphill. Turn left at a stile, PUBLIC FOOTPATH. Continue on this broad, well defined path for the next 1.7 km (1 mile).

Reaching the road, turn right and continue to the car park.

Wellington Monument
At the time of writing, the monument was undergoing repair and visitors could not enter to climb to the viewing platform. However, it is an impressive sight. Located on the highest point in the Blackdowns, it was completed in 1854 and honours the Duke of Wellington, who took his title from the town below after his victories in the Peninsular War. The victor of Waterloo became Commander-in-Chief in 1827 and served as Prime Minister (1828-30) and Foreign Secretary (1834-35).

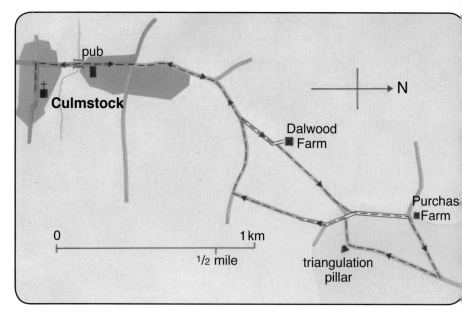

Walk 12   Culmstock Beacon

Distance: 5.3 km/3¹/₄ miles   Map 128
Character: From Culmstock Beacon (250 m/825 ft) a splendid vista
opens out. Embracing the Culm Valley, the Blackdowns, the Quantocks
and Haldon, it stretches to Dartmoor. The Beacon's unique beehive hut
dates from the Armada of 1588, when it was one of a chain of fire
beacons across southern England to give early warning of the Spanish
fleet. There is one steady ascent and a steeper descent.

Park carefully on the street by the church, noted for its beautiful
medieval priest's cope and the yew that grows from the top of the
tower. With your back to the main gate and south porch, turn right.
Turn right down TOWN HILL. Continue past the war memorial, over
the bridge and past the Culm Valley Inn, its sign and period photographs souvenirs of the Culm Valley Line that ran 7¹/₂ miles from
Tiverton to Hemyock.

   When the road bends sharp left continue ahead (HUNTER'S HILL)
past the school. Bear right when the lane curves sharp left. Turn left
(PUBLIC FOOTPATH) up a farm track. Cross the stile on your right and
continue uphill through the field to a stile on the far side. Continue
uphill as signed, passing to the right of the silage pits, then keeping the
hedge and wall just on your left.

26

Leave by a steel gate at the top corner. Follow the enclosed path ahead to a footpath junction. Turn left, PUBLIC FOOTPATH. Continue past a house to Purchas Farm. Fork right and uphill. Turn sharp right, almost doubling back, onto a broad, unsigned path. Continue to the triangulation pillar and beehive hut. Plaques explain the history of both hut and pillar.

With your back to the hut, follow the steep path downhill to a track. Turn left. Reaching a path junction, turn right, PUBLIC FOOTPATH. Follow the track downhill. At another junction, turn right along the lane. Reaching the junction with the farm track on your right, simply retrace your steps to the start.

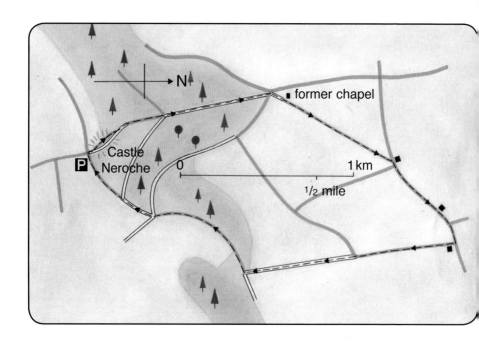

former chapel
Castle Neroche
P
0   1 km
1/2 mile

Walk 13   Castle Neroche

Distance: 5km/3 miles   Map 128
Character: Sited on the northern edge of the Blackdown escarpment,
Castle Neroche is a superb viewpoint with extensive ramparts. It has
a long and varied history. First an Iron Age hill fort, later a Norman
motte and bailey castle, it was refortified with a stone tower during the
'Anarchy' of the mid-12th century, when King Stephen and his cousin
Matilda vied for the English throne. Following woodland paths, quiet
lanes and tracks, this walk includes one short, steep ascent.

A variety of walking routes start from the car park, where a plaque
describes two. The route described here combines features from both.
Take the bridleway, HEREPATH. Bear left 10m ahead (HEREPATH) and
walk up onto the ramparts. Enjoy the views and walk on through the
centre of the ramparts, where a plaque gives more of Neroche's history.

At the junction with East Deane Way, continue ahead, HEREPATH,
following the blue bridleway arrows as the path descends from the
steep banks. Generations have trod this route: 'herepath' is an Old
English term dating from the 9th century describing a military road

developed in the struggle against Viking invaders. Naturally, herepaths were extensively used by ordinary people too.

At the next path junction continue ahead, HEREPATH. Meeting a road, turn right. Cross the lane junction 50 m ahead and turn immediately right into a track, PUBLIC FOOTPATH.

Follow the track to a stile by a former chapel. Follow the left field edge to another stile. Cross and continue with the field on your right through two fields and over stiles. Aim for the metal gate in the top left corner of the third field.

Continue with the hedge on your left to a lane. Turn right, ignoring the first lane right 40 m ahead. Take the second lane right. When the lane bends sharp right, continue ahead up a grassy track.

Turn right at a path junction. Follow the bridlepath uphill through trees. Reaching a path junction, continue ahead, CASTLE NEROCHE. When the track divides, keep left uphill – the path's steepness proves the defensive value of this site. Keep left as signed when the track divides again and climb onto the ramparts. Follow the path back to the car park.

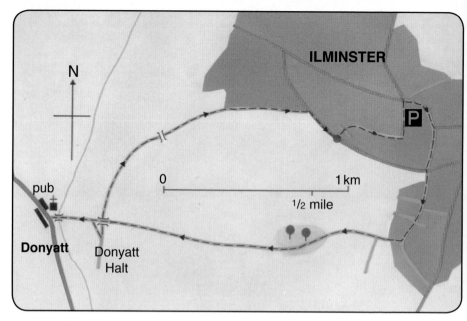

Walk 14   Ilminster

Distance: 5.9 km/3 3/4 miles   Map 128
Character: There is much of interest on this fairly gentle walk:
Ilminster's splendid church, the pretty Ham stone village of Donyatt
and a section of the former Taunton/Chard branch railway. This
includes bridges and cuttings, the remains of the Chard Canal and the
restored Donyatt Halt, with its World War Two defences, part of the
Taunton Stop Line designed to contain a German invasion of the South
West.

Turn right out of West Street car park. Follow West Street as it bends right into Silver Street and bends left towards the minster. Built of golden Ham stone, the minster is particularly noted for its 27 m (90 ft) tall tower, its magnificent tower crossing and brass monuments. Turn right opposite the minster into narrow WHARF LANE.

Reaching a T-junction by Muchelney House, cross the road ahead by traffic lights. Turn left and almost immediately right into ORCHARD VALE.

Follow ORCHARD VALE past playing fields and uphill through a housing estate. After passing Walrond Court on your left, take the next turn right into a cul-de-sac. At the end of the street walk down a ramp to a track junction.

Continue ahead (DONYATT) on an enclosed path with good views of Ilminster and the Isle Valley. Ignore side turnings and continue uphill through the wood. The path levels and then descends to a kissing gate.

Continue ahead on the field path with the hedge on your left and on into an enclosed path to a tarmac track. This passes over a railway bridge and a river bridge into Donyatt.

Divert right to visit St Mary's. Enter through the massive door, with its medieval hinges. Inside are Tudor bench ends, a Jacobean pulpit and an ancient chest.

Either turn right at the main road junction for the George Inn or retrace your steps immediately over the river bridge. Just before reaching the railway bridge, bear right, PUBLIC BRIDLEWAY.

Divert right to see Donyatt Halt. A plaque explains the history of the branch railway and wartime evacuees at Donyatt.

Follow the railway path under the bridge, ILMINSTER. Continue through Donyatt cutting, under another bridge and back to Ilminster.

Reaching a road, turn right ILMINSTER. Follow the pavement to a roundabout. Turn left, LOWER MEADOW. Continue ahead into a tarred footpath. Bear right and follow the path with the stream on your left. Reaching a path junction, turn left and uphill. Follow the path on up a side street past the theatre. Turn right into WEST STREET.

Canal walks from Taunton

Start from Tone Bridge in the centre of Taunton, built in 1895 and decorated with the town arms, with dolphins and scallop shells on the lamp standards.

Follow the riverbank path west (GOODLAND GARDEN) for 250 m. Divert left to see Taunton Castle. Originally the medieval castle of the Bishops of Winchester, Taunton Castle bears marks from the Royalist siege of 1644-45. It now houses the Museum of Somerset.

Return to the river. Cross the footbridge and continue on the north bank to leafy FRENCH WEIR PARK and the more expansive green space of LONGRUN MEADOWS. The footpath may be followed out of Taunton to more open countryside. At Bishops Hull it joins the West Deane Way, which stretches to Tiverton and beyond.

Alternatively, head east from Tone Bridge past THE BREWHOUSE THEATRE and SOMERSET CRICKET GROUND to Firepool Weir, where the Tone meets the Bridgwater & Taunton Canal. The towpath may be walked to Bridgwater (22.5 km/14 miles), but it does not enter open country until passing under the M5, 3 km/2 miles further on.